LIVE RESPONSIBLY, DIE THOUGHTFULLY

___ How to Navigate the Rest of Your ___
Life with Intention and Grace

Johanna Munson

Live Responsibly, Die Thoughtfully: How to Navigate the Rest of Your Life with Intention and Grace

By: Johanna Munson

ISBN for Print: 979-8-9908541-2-3

For permissions, contact: hello@johannamunson.com

Cover design: Rhianon Paige

Editing: Dustin Dixon

Published by: AFGO Press

Printed in the United States

First Edition 2024

NOTICE: The information provided in this book is not to be construed as a substitute for medical advice or professional services of any kind. It is for educational purposes only. Neither the author nor the publisher make any representations or warranties, express or implied, about the accuracy, completeness, reliability, suitability, or availability with respect to the information, products, services, or related materials contained in this book for any purpose. The advice and strategies contained herein may not be suitable for your particular situation. Any use of this information is at your own risk.

In order to maintain confidentiality and ensure privacy, the author has used aliases, changed identifying details, and created composite stories based on a variety of clients with whom she has interacted.

To the beloveds who have come before us;

To the ongoing chain of humanity;

To all of us who live, love, and ultimately die;

And to those beyond the veil.

TABLE OF CONTENTS

BEFORE WE GET STARTED...

Dear Reader,

Before we start, I want to congratulate you for your courage in picking up this book. Not everyone has what it takes to do that, believe me. I wouldn't have taken that step myself were it not for what I went through with the deaths of my parents.

I put off writing about my experiences for years, unwilling to revisit the pain and difficult feelings that surrounded my mom's end of life in 2007. Losing my dad in 2019 was another blow, and it took a number of years before I knew I could write from the scar, so to speak, and not from the wound.

In the coming pages, I'll introduce you to my Living Responsibly Roadmap and show you how coming to

1

terms with the inevitable yet somehow unimaginable fact of our mortality can lead to living an incredibly rich and fulfilling life, right up until the end.

To understand how (and why) you might resist this topic, I invite you to go to www. livingresponsiblyroadmap.com and download my free (and insightful!) Living Responsibly Quiz.

This book was born out of the contrast between the anguish and deep grief I felt about my mom's death and the relative calmness and acceptance of my dad's. I hope that my story will inspire you to make the choice to live responsibly and die as thoughtfully as possible.

In peace,

Johanna Munson
July 2024

INTRODUCTION

A Responsible Exit

My mother died irresponsibly.

I know that may sound harsh. But the truth is, if my mother had taken steps to die *thoughtfully*, I believe that my father, my sisters, and I would have suffered a whole lot less than we did.

Losing my mother at age 74 was devastating. We lived in the same town and had finally gotten to a place where we thoroughly enjoyed our relationship. I was looking forward to many more years of simply spending time with her and my dad.

I was heartbroken, and so were my sisters. My father was a wreck. Looking back, I wish things could have been different in so many ways.

I wish she hadn't died, of course.

But I also wish that she had taken care of things *before* she died. That she had died thoughtfully.

If only she had…

The possibilities haunted me for a decade.

⁂

I vividly remember the day we left the hospital after my mother died. The July sun was bright and cheerful, in stark contrast to the dark despair we were feeling. We walked in numb silence to the parking lot, and the reality that my mom would never walk with us again hit hard. I couldn't even look at my sisters, much less my dad, without bursting into tears. The "what ifs" began to cycle through my mind, and the guilt and regret wasted no time in rearing their ugly heads.

We had only five weeks from her diagnosis to her death. How does that even happen?! And why didn't she ever talk about what she wanted? By the time she ended up in the ICU, it was too late; all we could do was take turns singing childhood songs to her, hoping she knew we were there for her in the only way possible at that time.

The songs covered the awkwardness that was

developing between me and my sisters. We were already disagreeing about what route to take as her sudden decline worsened. Our dad didn't join us in singing as he was in shock: how could his beloved Faith be leaving him?

The shock of losing a loved one is to be expected.

But what most of us don't expect is the shock that comes with not knowing what to do next, especially when we end up fighting with our loved ones over "what she would have wanted."

It would have been so much better if she had *told* us what she wanted.

My sisters and I ended up turning *against* each other when what we needed most was to turn *toward* each other instead.

Fast forward 12 years to February 9, 2019, the day my dad died.

Walking home through the unusually deep snow with my younger sister by my side, the feelings of peace and acceptance were forefront. We knew that we had done our utmost to accompany our dad through his last weeks, doing our best to follow his wishes. The tears would also come, but they were tears of pure grief, untinged by feelings of remorse. He had lived responsibly and died thoughtfully, and the contrast with my mom's death couldn't have been stronger.

Very few of us actually want to talk about death and dying, and I was in that place myself after my mom's death. My dad grieved deeply for several years, and as he came out of that dark place, he started wanting to talk about his own end-of-life decisions. I resisted, still triggered by the experience with my mom.

I couldn't even *think* about losing my dad.

Reality intruded, however, and I was called upon to act as his medical and financial powers of attorney. He experienced a variety of health challenges, and we had deep and meaningful conversations about what was to happen next. The impact of being able to talk about what truly *mattered to him*, along with getting his affairs in order ahead of time, formed the foundation for creating what I now call the *Living Responsibly Roadmap* for fostering peace of mind at a time when life is vulnerable to chaos.

It's not like he said the quiet part out loud ("my wife didn't take responsibility"), but in retrospect, I can see that the feeling of helplessness and the trauma that he experienced made him determined to break the mold and do it differently himself.

The Living Responsibly Roadmap has 4 parts that

are intentionally designed to help us work through the most unavoidable event of our lives. That event, one that hopefully comes later rather than sooner, is the fact that we are all going to pass on someday.

But what do we do in the meantime?

How do we live responsibly?

And perhaps, even more critically (if we are to consider the feelings of our loved ones), what would you have to do now to ensure that you die *responsibly*?

The Living Responsibly Roadmap helps us remove the blinders and make decisions we don't want to think about making. It reveals an actual truth: None of us wants to die, leaving our loved ones burdened by decisions we could have made for them.

You are not alone in wanting to avoid thinking about this stuff! Very few of us want to spend time thinking about this inevitability.

And yet… who among us wants to inflict more suffering?

What makes us think that if we *ignore it*, things will work themselves out? Is it fair to tell ourselves that once we die, we won't have to deal with the heartache (and mess) of those we leave behind?

Is that really how we want to let things play out?

Wouldn't you rather step out of denial and into a place of responsibility, where we show how much we care *by taking care of our own affairs*? That's what it means to die thoughtfully.

Remember that awkward part of science class where you learned about the birds and the bees? I'm willing to bet there was no corresponding talk about the other end of the life cycle. We are not taught how to address illness, aging, dying, and death; the focus is all on youth and vitality.

In this book, I'll share my Living Responsibly Roadmap that empowers you to embrace your mortality and see it as a pathway to living fully now. I'll introduce my signature program, *Experience Peace of Mind Now*, where you're guided to create a personal roadmap that leads to peace of mind for you and those you love. You'll stop worrying so much about others because you'll know that they'll be taken care of when the unimaginable happens.

What's unique about my approach to tackling the often-daunting list of action items that others tell us need to be checked off (often referred to as "getting our affairs in order")? I do have a checklist that we use to identify our priorities, but we start by looking at who and what matters to us and how the way our life is going now reflects that (or not!). The checklist covers three areas that I call the Heart, Soul, and Mind of planning.

And there's so much more. You'll learn how to have deeply meaningful conversations on challenging topics, a skill that will serve you in many areas of life.

You'll deepen your relationships with yourself and others.

Imagine finding joy in every day, even with the ups and downs of modern life, confident that you are making the most of your "one wild and precious life" (from Mary Oliver's poem "The Summer Day").

Are you intrigued but still hesitant to venture into this unexplored territory? I get it. As I said, we're not necessarily taught how to navigate these pathways.

Sometimes it is forced upon us when we get an unexpected diagnosis or a loved one suddenly needs our help. It's a struggle to deal with the emotional and physical fallout when we don't have any planning in place.

But if we stay stuck here, we forego the opportunity to expand the depth of our being beyond where we are now, and we won't reap the benefits of inner exploration.

Take a moment to consider these questions:

Who am I when I have to let go of "doing"? (Getting old or experiencing severe illness means a whole lot of letting go!)

How can I prepare so that I am ready when that time comes? (Life gets busy and we think we can put off that task.)

What if I'm scared? (That's normal, and I'm here to help dispel your fears.)

Leaving those questions unanswered means missing out on a fundamental piece of being human. I am passionate about engaging with you at this level, and I am so deeply grateful to my parents and the lessons I learned from them that put me on the path to becoming a Peace of Mind Guide. I have personally experienced the peace of mind that planning provides, and I wish that everyone could feel that sense of ease.

You're not the only one if you've never considered that there is more to estate planning than creating a will or trust, deciding who gets what, and maybe getting a Health Care Directive in place. Between not knowing who to turn to and potential costs, it's no wonder people put this off! While 64% of Americans believe it's important to have a will, less than 40% of people over the age of 40 have actually put one in place (caring.com survey).

To go beyond that and pay attention to who and what we care about and how to live and die responsibly so that we leave this lifetime with as few regrets as possible: now that's transformative!

Do you want to continue to go about your daily life tied to the ways of thinking that keep you from living the full life you really want? Feeling like the other shoe could drop at any time but unwilling to take action? Missing out on connections, fulfillment, and really knowing who you are?

Why would you want to give up on all that potential joy?!

Believe me, I was severely depressed and in a horrible place after my mom died. I felt like I had lost so much; the conversations, the experiences, even the disagreements. It makes sense, right? I expected that she would live until at least 91, the age that her mom died.

Her death gave me the gift of awareness, but acceptance of my own mortality didn't come until I walked alongside my dad through his final days.

In the next chapter, I'll share how that attitude developed and how it got me to this place where I can bring you along with me through the Living Responsibly Roadmap.

It's time to take responsibility for your life and your eventual death. Avoidance of the latter will only continue to impede the former.

But it doesn't have to.

Let's find out why.

THE LIVING RESPONSIBLY ROADMAP

I had dropped by the yoga studio to make arrangements for my next workshop series, and coming out the door was a woman I'll call Jennifer. I'd crossed paths with her several times over the last 6 months, and every time, she'd say, "Oh, I need to talk with you, but I'm just not ready!"

This from an 80-year-old widow living on her own!

She'd told me she had nothing in place: no will or advance directive and two beloved cats that her nearby daughter had already said she couldn't take in. She was in denial at the age of 80, unwilling to say the hard part out loud: *I don't want to think about my own death.*

If you don't choose to live *responsibly*, you will die

irresponsibly.

This is what it looks like to live responsibly and die *thoughtfully* in the context of my framework:

- We make a conscious choice to lean into the reality of our mortality.

- We utilize that awareness to bring our lives into alignment with our core values.

- We put a roadmap in place for now until the end, thereby giving us the best chance of dying without regrets.

Dying thoughtfully is one of the greatest gifts we can give to ourselves *and* our loved ones, even though the mere thought of dying makes us want to turn away from the topic entirely.

Here's why: The death of a loved one is sure to cause pain and suffering for those still living. But what no one wants is to have what happens in the days or weeks leading up to their death *add* to that suffering, which is exactly what happened to our family when my mother got ill so suddenly.

No one in my family could agree on the decisions that had to be made after my mother's diagnosis and sudden decline, and that created a divide among family members. After her death, we struggled to put together a memorial service that would do justice to her incredible artistic spirit. I know my mother would not have wanted that, but she also failed to prevent it by not having made those decisions herself long before she died, when she was of sound mind and spirit.

Whenever I explain this to someone, they immediately experience a shift in perspective.

Instead of anticipating the grief and suffering their death will cause, they envision the possibilities for connection and fulfillment that being responsible *now* provides.

I've felt that pain, and it took me to a really dark place. Not only had I lost my mom, but my dad was in a state of shock and disbelief and needed a lot of support at the same time that I was suffering. My kids saw their grandmother once at the hospital, and the next thing they knew, she was gone.

Trying to explain death to a 9- and 12-year-old complicated matters further.

Her unexpected diagnosis of acute leukemia was such a surprise. She'd always been a go-getter, active in many organizations (including volunteering with hospice). There were only five weeks from diagnosis to her end of life, leaving us all in shock, and no one knew what she would have wanted before there were no more choices to be made. We'd never had the conversations that could have brought us all together at the end instead of causing enormous strain. Irresponsible? I would say yes.

It was so different with my dad, as he took that experience to heart and tried to initiate conversations with me about his choices. I resisted at first as I was still feeling deep regrets about the way my mom's end of life had gone. I was putting responsibility on myself for something that was hers to manage.

It became obvious as he aged, however, that putting all the pieces in place and laying out a hoped-for roadmap was a huge gift that he could give my sisters and me. The lessons I learned formed the foundation for my Living Responsibly Roadmap. Think about it: wouldn't you rest easier knowing that you've gained this awareness and that it can impact not only you but all those who care about you?

I know death is a taboo topic in dominant American culture. Moreover, the human brain is wired for survival and shouts, "No, don't go there!"

We think that if we avoid talking about it, we won't have to deal with it. Or that talking about it will make it happen sooner. Or that we don't need to do anything about it because we'll be dead.

If you have looked into planning for it, maybe you purchased a binder that has tabs for each subject, and now it's sitting in the drawer, still blank. Or you went to a presentation and picked up some business cards but tossed those a week or two later.

Without the foundational steps of my framework, you'll likely put off taking action again. The result? Those around you won't know what to do should you experience illness or death unexpectedly. And worst of all? You're likely to wind up living a life that is so much smaller than what is possible when you take full responsibility for both living *and* dying.

Have you experienced the death of a relative or close friend, where little preparation was done, and there was incredible strain placed on everyone? That might inspire you to examine your situation and think, "I don't want that to happen to those that I love!" Following this roadmap will spare your loved ones that awful experience.

Or maybe you saw the opposite situation, where the end of life was a sacred event, and community was created by the passing. It led to deeper connections and a profound awareness that life is precious. You want this for yourself and don't want to waste any more time but are not sure how to proceed. Deciding to be responsible in both life and death is key.

Of course, you don't want to make your passing even more difficult for your loved ones. If you did, you wouldn't have picked up this book in the first place.

Who wouldn't want to ease the path for those who will grieve for you after you're gone? And it's not just about those around you: imagine the sense of accomplishment that comes with tackling such a critical yet often-ignored topic. The bonus is that you get to reap the rewards of this expanded awareness of the precious nature of life.

Note: The Living Responsibly Roadmap is not for you if you're thrilled with your life as it is now, you think you have plans in place, and you don't see any need to expand your understanding of what is possible.

Granted, it's not easy to venture into this territory. Imagining a world without us in it can strike terror into the bravest of us. Missing out on important milestones, not achieving the goals we set, or enduring hardship because of illness are all legitimate fears. It takes guided focus to develop your capacity to get beyond the anxiety to a peaceful place where you have a clear roadmap to follow.

In that peaceful place, you'll understand that this is the best gift you can give your loved ones and yourself! You'll see clearly what matters to you the most and will know what steps to take to create a life that brings you joy, connection, and serenity.

My Living Responsibly Roadmap has four steps, and it's critical to take sufficient time to address each one.

Step 1: Conquering Avoidance

"I don't want to think about my death."

Does reading that sentence ring true?

It's no wonder that it does. Our brains are focused on keeping us alive, so even the thought of dying is an existential threat.

It is fundamental to acknowledge that this is a topic that we are reluctant to address, however, and our thoughts tend towards the following:

- I hate thinking about the time leading up to my passing.

- I don't want to think about me dying and my children/partner/siblings/parents having to live on without me.

- I don't even know what to think about "what's next" after death.

- I avoid talking about it because I'm scared that will make it happen.

- Occasions that should be happy are clouded by my fears.

- I don't take actions that could lead me to a fulfilling life because the risks are too great.

Do any of these resonate with you?

Whether it's what loved ones will do without me, or how I'll get through the end of my life, or some other concern, it's easier in the short term to avoid the subject altogether. But that can lead to unwanted outcomes for you and those around you.

"The terror of death is the underlying power that drives all human behavior." ~Ernest Becker

Step 2: Overcoming Resistance to Our Mortality

"I am going to die someday."

It is in the nature of all living things to die. When I can overcome my resistance to that reality, I gain the freedom to be fully present in my life. Making decisions becomes easier because I am aware of the fact that my time is limited. If not now, when?

Opposition to this unfortunate fact is deeply embedded in our subconscious brain, however. Thousands of years of human experience rewarded those who were able to stay alive, and our ancestors did that by seeking pleasure, avoiding pain, and conserving energy. Not much room for talking about death and dying in there!

When you stop fighting the inevitable, however, you

start to feel some freedom, believe it or not. Which would you rather experience: a constricted life where you're not taking risks, or one of expansion because you recognize that your time here is limited?

"Even death is not to be feared by one who has lived wisely." ~Buddha

Step 3: Becoming Accountable

"How do I want to live my life now so that I have no regrets later?"

Of course, no one wants to get to the end of their life and feel regret, but how often do we take steps to ensure we die without deep remorse for not living responsibly and dying *thoughtfully*?

Consider asking yourself these questions also:

- What do I have to do now so that I can rest assured that my loved ones will be taken care of?

- How can I make my wishes clear?

And this question, perhaps the most important one of all:

- How do I hold myself accountable for what I say I want?

This isn't only about taking care of your loved ones; it's about taking care of *you*. And when you take responsibility for the things that matter to you, you end up taking care of the ones you love.

When you take personal responsibility for living your life *now* in ways that ensure both you *and* your loved ones are taken care of, everyone benefits. You get to drop the weight of worrying about them when you're no longer here, and they understand your choices. You're living your life consistent with the values that matter most to you.

We routinely take on responsibility for others' lives, so why is it often challenging to transform our own? We may raise kids, we try to satisfy our boss, and we are often called upon to ease the path for a partner or friend. When we understand the impact of our choices (by the way, avoidance is a choice, too), we can shape our destiny.

No more blaming others or making excuses. Once you're taking responsibility for your life, you become the architect of your future.

Identifying our values provides a solid foundation for making all kinds of decisions and allows us to take ownership of our lives.

"Have the courage to build your life around what is really most important to you." ~Joshua Becker

STEP 4: Living Responsibly

"What will give me peace of mind?"

Imagine yourself here: you're no longer wasting energy resisting the fact of your mortality, and you're ready to explore what living life fully means for you.

You no longer live with the worry that your loved ones won't be taken care of after you're gone. Picture them knowing how to support you as you age, prepared for emergencies because of the conversations you've had. Some of us are "solo agers" and need to plan for a circle of caring. What a relief it would be to have that in place!

You've made your healthcare and other choices before it's an emergency situation, resulting in peace of mind for you and those around you. And when the end comes, it's not a disaster; it's a sacred event.

It may seem counterintuitive that focusing on your end of life can completely transform your present situation, but these are some of the results my clients have had:

One woman was still working at age 70, and through completing this process, realized that she could retire and travel as she had always dreamed.

I worked with a couple, leading busy lives with

teenage daughters and facing an empty nest, who recommitted to their partnership as they fully took in that life can change in an instant and now is all they have.

Communication was enhanced in another partnership as they overcame differences of opinion. Now they have a structure for handling difficult topics!

You're accustomed to taking responsibility for so many areas of *living* and take great pride in that.

But you probably haven't thought about the costs of *dying* irresponsibly.

» Dying irresponsibly means you didn't really take care of yourself (and your loved ones) when you were still living and had the opportunity to put your affairs in order.

» Dying irresponsibly means you'd "rather not think about it," even if it causes tension within the family before *and* after you're gone.

» Dying irresponsibly means you fail to consider the pain you leave behind.

» Dying irresponsibly means you create unnecessary suffering for your loved ones.

» Dying irresponsibly means you don't get to

live your life to the fullest extent possible right now.

The first step in learning how to live and die responsibly is explained on the next page.

Come along with me, and let's take a deeper look at each step. I promise you, it's not all doom and gloom. In fact, there's no doom and gloom whatsoever when you learn how to *think* responsibly.

Get ready to be inspired!

"It is not the end of the physical body that should worry us. Rather, our concern must be to live while we're alive - to release our inner selves from the spiritual death that comes with living behind a facade designed to conform to external definitions of who and what we are." ~Elisabeth Kubler-Ross

STEP 1:

Conquering Avoidance

"I don't want to think about my death."

I would have been the first to say NO! if asked, "Would you like to talk about death and dying today?"

What a strange question that is. *Of course, I don't want to even think about dying, much less have a conversation about it.*

But *thinking* responsibly means we don't shirk things just because they make us feel uncomfortable.

How often do we take time to consider the unintended consequences of ignoring the reality that we are mortal? For most people, that doesn't hit home until we come face to face with death. Most of us don't want to die, at least not right this moment.

*If you are having thoughts of suicide, please contact the 988 Suicide and Crisis Lifeline by texting "help" to 988 or going to www.988lifeline.org.

Have you ever had a near escape in a car accident? A frightening health scare? Or the experience of these things happening to someone you care about? Then you know what I'm talking about. In those moments, awareness of the desire to live fully while we're here becomes our entire focus and can be the catalyst that impacts our lives forever after.

But there's no reason to wait until something traumatic happens. That's why Conquering Avoidance is Step 1 in my framework. Think of it as an invitation to step onto a new path, to choose the fork in the road that leads to clarity instead of confusion.

Now, I recognize that there's very little guidance provided. Death is not a common topic at the dinner table; at least, it wasn't in my family!

Even in medical school, students spend very little time learning how to discuss dying and death and don't get a chance to develop the necessary skill set in talking about it unless they specialize in palliative or hospice care. If they're not able to discuss it, why would I be?

No, I didn't want to think about dying, but I was unaware of how that impacted my life until I'd gone through the loss of both of my parents.

I'd experienced a few deaths of people close to me when my mom's diagnosis surprised us all. I know for sure now that her death would not have been so traumatic if she'd talked with us more openly. We had some time before she entered the hospital for chemotherapy, a brief moment when she was aware of her mortality but still not willing to go there with me, my dad, and my sisters. But we also could have started the conversations well before that crisis.

I remember the doctor gave her a 50/50 chance that the chemo would work. We all focused on the "glass half full" part of those odds, understandably.

The first round didn't work, however, and her health continued to decline. I can picture, even now, the last time that I saw her outside of the ICU. She wanted to feel the warm July sun on her face, so I got her up to the rooftop garden of the hospital in a wheelchair.

My heart was breaking that my beloved mom, usually so active and strong, could no longer walk. But even faced with such stark evidence that a full recovery wasn't likely, we stuck to "safe" topics like what was blooming in her garden at home and how my kids were doing.

Unwilling to even admit the possibility that she would never again plant new flowers in that garden or see her beloved grandkids grow up, she wasn't able to take responsibility in that moment. Ideally, we would have addressed this possibility well before this point, but that was an opportunity lost.

She just didn't want to admit she was stuck in Step One, "I don't want to think about dying."

And I didn't have any clue as to how to go there with her.

You may be thinking, "That's unfair to expect your mom to be able to talk about her own end of life when she's focused on her treatment," and you'd be right. That was not the time to do that work! We might have taken the time to go deeper when she got the diagnosis, but even that would have put a lot of pressure on us as a family. And she really didn't expect that this would be the end.

Getting beyond societal norms is hard, I get it.

But you can't change and grow if you stay stuck in a place that's not serving you. You may unconsciously believe that breaking the "rules" and actually talking about end-of-life topics will put people off. Thoughts of "what will they do without me" may be so painful that you *think* you can't go there.

Or maybe you've seen others shift their beliefs and develop the capacity to address the inevitable, but that feels out of reach for you.

Thinking responsibly takes practice, especially when it *feels* uncomfortable.

Becoming aware of your unconscious thought patterns is the first step to taking responsibility for your evolution into a person living your life to the fullest now. Why put off this crucial move and continue living a life of fear and avoidance, remaining subject to the chances of fate and only addressing mortality in a crisis situation? I know that you are capable of stepping out on this path, and I'm here to be your guide.

What is one of the first things that comes to mind when you hear that someone died and has surviving family members? For me, after conveying my heartfelt condolences, it would be, "What about a will? Did they have a valid one? And what's going to happen to all their stuff?"

Here's a story I'd like to share. My good friend Allen is one of three sons, and one of those sons lived with their aging father (along with his girlfriend) in the father's home. This arrangement worked for many years, but there were no formal details laid out, such as compensation for caregiving or any mention of rent. This friend saw his father's health declining and tried to get access to any kind of documentation but was met with resistance on all fronts, including from his dad.

When their beloved father died, the son who had taken care of him refused to move out of the home, citing all the "free" care he had provided. It turns out that there was a trust, but the lawyer who created it had retired and moved to Florida, and the bank where the trust was held refused to cooperate as no estate executor had been named. It cost this friend $40,000 in lawyer fees and a year of delays to sort it all out. In the meantime, relationships fell apart, and the former caregiving son had to be evicted.

This is a classic case of a parent not choosing to take responsibility while alive, thus creating a huge mess for his family at his death. Imagine a different scenario: the dad was aware that he needed help and honored his sons by recognizing the unique contributions each could make. One was able to manage his finances, and another was there for him as a caregiver. Another son who lived far away made it a point to call his dad every week on Sunday and talk about the latest baseball stats.

The father took time to create an estate plan, and when he died, everything was settled according to his wishes, and the family came together to honor him with love in their hearts. It inspired them to connect more often virtually as they live in different states, deepening their relationships as they are now heart-wrenchingly aware that time rushes on.

Which of these scenes do you prefer? If you continue to brush off Step 1, Conquering Avoidance, it's more than likely to look like the first. I've seen families with hurt feelings, holding onto long-lived resentments, and even cutting off contact, all because people were unwilling to shift long-held beliefs and patterns of behavior. But that was just their subconscious talking or society telling them what to do or not do.

Are you listening to that inner voice that says, "Stop! This isn't safe!"

If it's extreme, you might feel like you're panicking and unable to even take a breath. If that's happening to you, stomp your feet on the ground a few times to re-establish that you're alive and ok. Go ahead, do it!

Maybe it's telling you that you just don't have what it takes to bust out of complacency and reach for new ways of being. Or that you don't have the courage to dive into your beliefs and challenge what's not working for you.

Do you resonate with any of these statements?

"No one around me is talking about this, so I'm not going to either."

"My family is too stuck in their ways, and I'd be the odd one out."

"I read something about this online, but it frightened me, so I closed the tab!"

If you're unaware that these kinds of messages are running your life, what else could you be missing out on? When you conquer avoidance of this incredibly challenging topic, you open the door to an entirely new way of being. In this world, you're on a voyage of self-discovery, with the potential for so many opportunities to come your way.

You can't move on to Step 2, Overcoming Resistance, however, until you unearth and expose the invisible blocks that keep you in avoidance. That would be like expecting a baby to walk before it's developed the bone structure, the muscles, and the mental capacity to accomplish that feat. The baby can't do this on its own; it requires the parents to take responsibility and create the setting where this development can occur. In this case, you are the parent (whether you're one in real life or not), and it's up to you to create the right environment.

Before we progress to Step 2, I want to reassure you that it's not wrong to feel reluctant, fearful, or awkward about this first step towards taking responsibility for your life and, therefore, your death. Towards dying thoughtfully. You are one of many who experience these limiting emotions that can lead to a constricted, less-than-fulfilling life and perpetuate the patterns in generations to follow. We *can* learn to accept death as a natural part of the life cycle and discover beautiful lessons in the process.

Even if you think you've "got your affairs in order," that's only scratching the surface of what's possible when you're living a life free from those unconscious patterns that hold you back from dying thoughtfully.

Nothing changes until we do the inner work; effective outer action is the result of taking sufficient time to turn inward.

You can shift your inner awareness and let go of the resistance to facing reality, which is Step 2.

I am certain of that.

STEP 2:

Overcoming Resistance to Our Mortality

"I am going to die someday."

Do you know someone who seems to live an unusually drama-free life? That certainly wasn't me; I've been through estrangement from family members, divorce after a long-term marriage, several major surgeries (including having a benign tumor removed from my brain), financial ups and downs, and more. But when I came to terms with the fact that "I am going to die one day," all that drama fell away, and I could transform that pain into energy to move towards the life I really want to live.

That is the power of letting go of resistance to this fact of life. That's why it is the necessary Step 2 in this process. It really sets the foundation for allowing us to view our inevitable demise as motivation rather than crippling us so that we remain stagnant.

My family wasn't unusual in our avoidance of death as a topic of conversation, and I certainly experienced more than a few losses before my mom "crossed the bar." (There are more than 100 euphemisms for dying and death, which just shows how uncomfortable we are with the reality!)

A high school friend died of leukemia, and I remember sobbing at his funeral, but then we went back to life as usual. My grandfather had a stroke and was gone soon after, but my mom was the only one who attended his service. There was no opportunity for me and my sisters to process the loss. The worst was probably my dad's mom, whom we called "Boo." She had an open casket service led by the funeral home director, who had never met her before. She was laid out in an elaborate casket in her best tweed suit with full makeup on, looking nothing like herself. Talk about denial! She was never still in all the years I knew her, so it was a visceral shock to my system to see her lying there.

Have you had experiences like these, or heard stories where these losses were denied until reality set in, or were swept under the rug, or were treated like they hadn't even happened?

I know how hard it is to come to terms with dying and death and treat it as an inevitable and sacred life event rather than a tragedy. I could blame my resistance on that lack of acceptance in my family of origin, or on society for discouraging me from even considering the idea of alternate approaches. Some of us have religious or spiritual traditions that are supposed to provide a framework for acceptance but can end up confusing us even more.

We don't want to upset others by revisiting losses or be thought an oddball for trying to shift the narrative. As I said before, some may even think it hastens the end to talk about it. Not a risk any sane person would take!

But how is this inability to move towards accepting that "I am going to die" showing up in *your* life? You may think the effect is negligible, but in reality, it could cost you the life that you are meant to be living.

I'm serious, so please stay with me here.

In the introduction, I mentioned how, after my mom's death, the last thing I wanted to think about was losing my dad. He was eye-to-eye with his own mortality at that point, however, and I consider it a real blessing that he lived long enough and was so strong-willed that he brought me to that place alongside him.

Throughout those years, our connection deepened

even as he went through health challenges and surgeries. He had clarified his priorities and knew what quality of life meant to him. My role was to support him in living his best life, and I only came to do this work because of the impact that time had on me. He was living responsibly.

Contrast that with a hospice patient that I was assigned as a volunteer. He was 93 years old with severe dementia and living in memory care (which runs over $100,000 per year). Blind in one eye and unable to hear much, even with a hearing aid, he often wasn't even aware when his son visited. He was on multiple medications and bed-bound and often had to be sedated because of severe anxiety. The one thing I could do to bring some light to his days was to sing with him, and we had many rousing choruses of "Swing Low, Sweet Chariot."

This man no longer had any agency over his life, and his son held medical power of attorney, so was making all the decisions (and paying the bills). The patient finally refused to eat and drink, knowing somewhere in his being that it was his time to go.

What if he had been willing to acknowledge his mortality before his health deteriorated so much? His family will never know how things might have been different, but they're left with those images of him curled up uncomfortably in a hospital bed instead of at peace in the location he might have preferred.

This is why overcoming resistance to the idea of death as early as possible is so critical. The sooner you work through this process, the more time you will have to *live* responsibly before you "kick the bucket" responsibly.

What would you be doing if you knew that you had 3 months to live? What if it was 3 years? So many emotions arise in me when I picture the first scenario, and those have definitely shifted as I've come to an awareness of my mortality.

I would have panicked and been unable to consider my options before I did this work, but in this state of equanimity, I would drop what didn't matter to me and focus on making sure that my death would bring people together. If I had three years to live I might shift my focus to simplifying my life and spend my time volunteering, gardening, singing, dancing (as long as I am able!), and being with the people who matter most to me.

We experience loss all the time, whether it's a relationship, a role in life, possessions, or a capability. What matters to me is that how I live and die inspires others to accept that death can come at any time and that it is a natural part of the life cycle. On a personal level, it is critically important to me to have my final act, my death, be one that creates cherished memories and doesn't add unnecessary suffering for those I leave behind.

You have your own set of values that influence how you live your life each day. But have you developed a *conscious awareness* of these critical components of who you are at your essence? Many of us go through life a little blindly, trusting that we have a general sense of what matters to us. Those values become clear in a crisis, but at that point, it may be too late to take action that is in alignment with your true self.

What are you depriving yourself of? Are you missing opportunities to make a significant impact in areas that are important to you because you put off taking action? Isn't that similar to how you've avoided recognizing that your time in this body is limited?

- I'll do it next year!

- I'll wait until my kids are out of the house!

- When I get the new job/relationship/home, then I'll be ready!

If you refuse to accept that at some point, you will breathe your last breath, it's easy to put off looking too deeply at what that will mean to you (in terms of how you live your life now) and to those you love (who will experience unnecessary inconvenience and anguish because of your irresponsibility).

I've shared with you why it is key to expand your awareness of your thoughts about death first, and that's Step 1. In that step, you developed insight into your reaction to the concept of death. That might look like, "I don't want to hear the word death, much less think about it!" or even "Blah blah blah," and you stick your fingers in your ears.

Or it could be a slow realization that happens as your body ages, and you have to let go of more and more parts of you that were once your identity. "Death happens to others, and I kinda know it's out there somewhere waiting for me, but I'm not going there yet." Does that ring true for you?

It's a very grown-up thing to do, to move to this stage of acceptance of mortality. There may be events in your life that have forced you to take this leap, including major losses and trauma. I'm sorry for whatever pain you are experiencing. Sometimes, I don't want to be the one with all the responsibility. Are you with me there?!

Unless you step up to the plate and get real with the fact that life is a one-way ticket, however, you'll most likely continue to live a less-than-full existence. And you won't progress to the final level where you've taken personal responsibility for ensuring peace of mind for yourself and your loved ones.

Remember, avoiding the topics of illness, dying, and death is pretty much baked into mainstream culture in the U.S., so it's no wonder that it takes conscious effort to break out of that limiting belief system. I've shown you how staying stuck in avoidance can lead to horrible situations; remember that 93-year-old in memory care? And the discord and heartache in addition to debilitating grief around my mom's death, all because we weren't willing to go there?

Contrast that with the experience of closeness I had with my father, where we cherished the knowledge that we could talk about anything, large or small, life-changing or mundane. Because we both accepted that he would not be here forever, when the end came, we knew what to do and trusted each other.

He showed me what is possible when I am willing to access the courage that is within me and acknowledge and embrace what is inevitable for us all. It took me years to get to that point, and it is my honor to distill what I have learned into my Living Responsibly Roadmap and shorten the process for you.

You have the benefit of learning from my journey, and I am committed to showing you that you, too, can live responsibly and leave this world with a sense of "job well done."

Congratulations! Being willing to say "Yes, I am going to die" out loud is a huge step to take. If you're not quite there yet, go back and read the last two chapters. Pause and take a long slow breath, in and out, and see if you can recognize that tiny part of you that already knows. When you feel that awareness, imagine encouraging that part of you to expand a little and open up to new worlds of possibility.

When you're ready (and you may already be feeling a sense of freedom that I see in my clients when they get to this point), move on to Step 3, where we'll look at taking accountability for your life from now until the end, and beyond as well!

STEP 3:

Being Accountable

"How do I want to live my life now knowing my loved ones will be taken care of because my wishes are clear?"

I believe that we don't ask ourselves this question early enough in our lives. (Note: the term "loved ones" doesn't just mean biological family members; it includes chosen family as well.)

Life was going well for my mom when her sudden diagnosis happened. None of us expected that she would get ill at such an early age (her mom had lived until 91, so of course she was going to do the same!). She probably thought she still had loads of time to be intentional about her aging years and beyond. She ate well, exercised, was an accomplished artist, had a great social life and a strong marriage, so there

49

were no real risk factors that would have set off alarm bells.

At that time, we lived in the same town and enjoyed each other's company. Growing up, though, my relationship with my parents was complicated, to say the least. As a child, I was fed and clothed, given many opportunities to explore my interests, and was able to go to college with their help, so they both showed responsibility there.

But when it came to expressing emotions? Nope, not going there! I never heard or said "I love you" until I was leaving for college, and my heart pounded as I choked out the words. I made a conscious choice to tell my kids that at every opportunity: an example of the kind of mindset shift that is necessary to permanently change behaviors and outcomes. Because we had repaired our relationship, it's still hard for me to say out loud that my mom was irresponsible at the end of her life.

The truth is, even if your family and friends have the best intentions, the responsibility still lies with you.

Yes, *you*, a mortal being.

No attorney can make you create a will.

No person in your life is going to force you to live like you mean it.

The only force on earth that can make these things happen for you is *you*.

Read that sentence as many times as you need to.

Back to that ICU scene, where my sisters and I were arguing about the best course of action, and our dad was in shock, seemingly unable to process what was happening. Because she hadn't made her choices known to us before this all happened, we were left with only hard decisions to make. Decisions that could have been clear-cut if she had taken responsibility.

The end of life she experienced was most likely not what she would have wanted, but we'll never know. We didn't know how to support her because she never voiced those decisions.

Being a *responsible* adult can be overwhelming, I know. There is pressure to find work, meet a partner, get a house, maybe have kids. Along with those new roles, we take on many responsibilities without necessarily consciously *deciding* to take them on.

It's one thing to do things because we're expected to do them; it's quite another to say, "This is a responsibility I am deciding to take on because it is important to me, my family, and my life."

It's common to put off thinking about getting old

as it may be decades away. Why add more to your plate?!

When you're facing a transition such as empty nesting, a divorce or remarriage, or retirement, decision after decision has to be made. In any of these situations, it's easy to get "decision fatigue." As you get better at empowering yourself through your choices, however, you develop that "muscle" and can apply it to new areas. We just don't think of applying it to our mortality.

How strong is your decision-making muscle? I used to take my time researching all the options, getting others' opinions on matters that were really up to me to decide, and dithering about which way to go. Does that sound familiar?

I justified it by saying I wanted to be informed or I didn't want to make the wrong choice. By not taking personal responsibility for my own life, I ended up living according to what was best for others. Their opinions and voices mattered more than mine! Just seeing that in print makes me shudder.

After my mom's death, my father took personal responsibility for living his life in a way that ensured his daughters were provided for and that we knew his wishes for how he wanted to live out his life according to his values. Discussing these topics was not part of his life experience up to that point, but the necessity and benefits of doing so became crystal clear.

If I hadn't had that experience of guilt, anguish, and regrets after my mom passed, I might not have taken action to make sure that my own plans were in place.

No one can take this step for you, and that's actually good news! You are a unique individual and can choose what is right for you. When you develop your ability to take action in alignment with your values (who and what matters most to you), a mindset shift happens that affects all areas of your life.

We get caught up in what others think of us, or what "should" be, or limited by our inner voice telling us we're not good enough. I'm here to tell you that you are an amazing human being and assure you that taking this opportunity to up-level your awareness of that reality will have wide-ranging positive effects.

The best part? You'll live your life *now* knowing two things: first, that you are living "eyes wide open," clear on what's important to you, and second, that your loved ones will be taken care of when your time to go occurs, whether it's sudden and unexpected or decades from now.

Once again, a gentle reminder that *if you don't live your life responsibly, you'll die irresponsibly.*

Did you know that Picasso died without having anything in place in terms of what to do with his immense fortune?! You'd think that someone living that large a life would have considered how to handle his affairs and at least have made some arrangements. The list of famous people who died irresponsibly is shocking and includes Prince, Aretha Franklin, John Denver, Martin Luther King Jr, and so many more.

Their relatives spent years litigating the estates, resulting in strained relationships with severe financial consequences. Parents and children, siblings, partners and ex-spouses, all suffer from this kind of neglect, and the only ones who benefit are the lawyers. It's sad to think that their actual end of life was probably not the kind of transition they would have wanted.

These stories are all too common and can be completely avoided when you honor your commitment to yourself and those you love.

To be clear, I mean no disrespect when I say they died irresponsibly. I am quite confident that if they'd had a book like this to guide them, things would have been different.

Are you saying to yourself, "This is where I need to start. I got this. I'm aware of the finite nature of being human, and yes, I know that applies to me, too. I'm ready to tackle all the things that need to get done." Whoa, there, stay with me.

What happens when you gloss over Step 1, Conquering Avoidance, and Step 2, Overcoming Resistance? You'll run out of steam very quickly when it comes to creating the full experience of what is possible when you commit to living responsibly.

If you're not living responsibly, you're not expressing your true self. It's that simple.

Living responsibly does not mean always putting others' needs ahead of your own; that's not at all what I'm saying. As I stated earlier in this chapter, each of us is a unique human being, and so living responsibly will look different for each of us.

So often, people want a quick solution: "Give me a checklist, and I'll get right on it." How many of those checklists end up at the back of the file cabinet or buried in your computer files and never see the light of day? Probably most of them, if we're being honest.

We look for those "easy" routes because at least we feel like we're doing something, and that's good, right? However, taking actions that are not aligned with who you are at your core will never be fulfilling. Claiming ownership of your life is a transformative step to lasting change. You become the proactive architect of your future, creating the life you envision.

We'll get to the final step, creating the life you want to live before AND after you die, in the next chapter.

When I think back on my dad's last decade, I'm so impressed by his recognition of the reality that he could be accountable for his own life up until the end. The heartbreak we experienced with my mom was the catalyst for him to grow well into his 70s and 80s and finally get to Step 3, Being Accountable.

Are you starting to see how empowering it can be to view your mortality in light of opportunity rather than tragedy? Of course, we grieve when those we love are "called home." We'll never hold their hand again or laugh and cry with them, and that hurts at such a deep level.

Step 4 of my Roadmap is where the magic happens. You realize that, truly, now is all we have, and making the most of that is up to you.

Welcome to Living Responsibly!

STEP 4:

Living Responsibly

"What will give me peace of mind?"

I'll say it again: My mom died *irresponsibly*.

Contrast that with the responsible way my dad died. I can't overstate the incredible impact this has had on my life. You, too, can experience this peace of mind.

I would be in the place you might be in right now if it weren't for him acknowledging that he would "cross over."

I could still be living in denial and unaware of my own potential if I hadn't learned from his willingness to accept that reality rather than be paralyzed by it.

I wouldn't have the close relationships I've nurtured if I hadn't applied the lessons I learned from him about how precious our time here on our beloved planet Earth really is.

And most importantly, I now live a life of integrity.

Recognizing that he was the only one who could effectuate a different outcome, he insisted on us having these deeply meaningful conversations. But he had to do the internal work first.

It's your choice: you can choose to live *and* die responsibly, but it's up to you. Starting now is key, and it is not too late, even if you're in your 90s! If you still want to close this book and run away, go back to that first step and tell your lizard brain to calm down. You're not about to be eaten by a saber-toothed tiger!

So, what does Living Responsibly look like?

I share the story of my client Alison, to whom I posed this very question. She is in her 60s with no kids and a divorced husband who left the state but also left a bunch of his stuff in a garage and rental units on her property (the things we put up with!). She got occupied with her business and kept putting off dealing with the situation. Several health challenges led her to work with me as she was no longer able to ignore the *what-ifs*.

Two things were on Alison's mind: she needed those

around her now to know what to do if she was ever incapacitated or, worst case, "shuffled off this mortal coil," and she knew she didn't want to work forever and thus needed her ex's stuff out so that she could convert the outbuildings to rentals for passive income.

Guess what? She now has all of her affairs in order, affording her peace of mind. She worked with her former husband to clean out the junk and get renters in, so now she has a retirement plan in place. There was healing in doing that together, which was an unexpected bonus.

Taking action looks different for each person, but your roadmap becomes much clearer now because you've gone through the previous steps. You can see around more of the curves.

The integrity you've cultivated in Steps 1, 2, and 3 guides you to identify priorities and set goals that are aligned with your true self. You're no longer veering off the path on a whim or overly influenced by others' opinions of who you should be or what you should do. I hate those shoulds!

If this stage feels like a big leap to you, consider it as lengthening your stride and taking a bigger step forward. Tiptoeing through the rest of your life, trying to find your way on a path that you didn't create for yourself: is that really what your heart desires? It can be challenging to manage the competing needs of those around us, but ignoring our own needs and perpetuating that people-pleaser part of us will lead us down a dead-end. Literally!

You're ready for this step when you notice that your thoughts create positive feelings about yourself, your circumstances, and your choices. Yes, our thoughts do create our feelings, not vice versa. Life happens, and we think we have to react to it in certain ways. But learning how to manage our thoughts empowers us to make decisions that serve our highest good.

Are you feeling like you could use an "assist" right about now? Life can feel overwhelming and it's critical to our well-being as humans to have people who have our back.

Reaching out for support is a sign of self-awareness and strength, and I highly recommend you work with professionals like me who have traveled this highway and can see smooth sailing ahead.

Imagine that open road in front of you, one you envisioned, with signposts ready to guide you when the road forks or an unexpected curve shows up. Your sense of direction is strong because you took the time to reflect on what really matters to you and created your own unique markers.

You've got clarity and confidence and are living an

authentic life. What a beautiful place to be!

You may be tempted to try to design your roadmap and take actions to implement it without going through the first 3 steps, and you wouldn't be the first. Reaching that place of knowing how to design the path that is right for you is an evolutionary process, however.

When you conquer avoiding thinking about your own death (Step 1), you've developed the ability to face other challenges that may be scary. Without this fuel for your engine, however, you'll quickly run out of steam and go back to old habits of sidestepping or retreating on the idea of death and, oh my the way, ditto for other major issues.

Do you really want that?!

Opening your mind and heart to reality is the work we did in Step 2, Overcoming Resistance and accepting that someday, you don't know how or when, you are going to die. Stay with me here, as I know that can still feel really uncomfortable. But it is critical to come to terms with this fact so that you can shift to feeling inspired by that certainty instead of feeling powerless.

Now that you're motivated, you're at the point where you can embrace the reality that you are the only one on this planet who can take responsibility for you.

Not your partner, your parent, your adult child, or a good friend.

You, and *only you*.

That's Step 3, Being Accountable.

Yes! You can now look at what Living Responsibly means to you, which is Step 4!

Take a moment to reflect on what you were like before you picked up this book. Something about it caught your eye, and if you've gotten this far, that's a good sign that you are ready to get in the driver's seat and find out what Living Responsibly means for you personally. I guarantee it will be transformative in a way that is unique to who you are.

This is *you* taking responsibility for *your* future, the rest of your life from now until the end. You get to choose the goals that inspire you and prioritize what matters to you. You get to continue growing in dynamic ways that animate you. No more existing on auto-pilot or living someone else's version of life.

Like it or not, we all put roadblocks in our own way. I hate to admit it, but if my dad hadn't so clearly taken responsibility for his life, this huge obstacle might still be in my way.

I was divorced with full-time custody of a teenager

when his health began to decline. I was drifting about, trying to find my way in the world after being a full-time mom and part-time educator for two decades. I depended on others to provide for me, thinking that the roadmap my former husband and I had designed would go according to plan. He took a left turn, and I had no idea where I was headed.

It took going through the steps in this book for me to get to the point where I could set my own compass, and I've never been happier! I've also discovered unexpected talents. Because I'm in this arena of death and dying, where the veil is thin, I now hear from loved ones on the other side.

Yes, I realized that I am a medium!

What feelings rise up in you when you think about your life as you're living it now? Are you feeling anxious? Modern life is no joke. There's a heck of a lot going on in the wider world right now, not to mention what's right in front of us.

Maybe you're feeling confident about your work or family life but have a sense that something is missing, that there's more to being alive than what you have right now.

When you live responsibly, you develop an inner knowing of where to focus and energy. You're able to navigate obstacles without getting distracted. You live your life with integrity, feeling secure *because* you know that the end will come. When that happens, you die with few regrets.

How can I state this so unequivocally? Because I've seen it with my own eyes and not only with my dad.

What are the top regrets of the dying? Take a look:

- Not living a life true to oneself but following the expectations of others.

- Working too hard and not making time for family and friends.

- Not expressing one's feelings and saying 'I love you' more often.

- Losing touch with family and friends and not resolving conflicts.

- Not letting oneself be happier and enjoy life.

Now do you see why taking control of the steering wheel of your life matters? Only you can create the path that leads to happiness and enjoyment of life. That last one hits me deep in my heart, and I would deeply regret it if I neglected to pay attention to what brings me joy and happiness. It's not that my life is happy all the time, needless to say, but I can truly say that my overall experience is one of joy and contentment.

Of course, we have to take others into consideration. I'm not suggesting otherwise! We need others because we are social creatures, but it's not wrong to prioritize ourselves so that we have the wherewithal to support both ourselves and those we love.

Does this process take time and emotional energy? You bet it does. Creating transformation in our lives is not for the faint of heart. The end result? Peace of mind and the capacity to be fully present.

This step, Living Responsibly, is where your courage and determination inspire you to frame the rest of your life, from now until the end. This is where the rubber meets the road: the life you are living is the one you have created. You can take chances, knowing that your guideposts are in place and your vision inspires you. And you know deep inside that those you love will not suffer needlessly because you have taken this step.

Does all this effort apply to other areas besides end-of-life? I'm thrilled to share that you can utilize these steps in any part of your life where you desire transformation. There's nothing more threatening to the primitive part of our brain than the idea of extinction, so when you can deal with that reality, you can deal with anything!

When you live responsibly, you quiet that "lizard brain" and allow the highly-evolved sections of your brain to take over. You are aware of your thoughts and choose the ones you want to think, and this is a valuable skill to develop. You get to live that "drama-free" life that has you in charge: a life of integrity.

We are not taught how to live our lives this way, and it's taken me years of study, life experience, and twists and turns to get to this place myself. It is an honor to have this opportunity to be your guide.

I get chills up and down my spine when I reflect on the transformations my clients have experienced, and I've shared some of their stories here. What do you want your narrative to be? Will you never step onto the road that you create intentionally but rather continue to live in denial?

If that doesn't appeal to you and you're ready to take charge of your destiny, let's contemplate your next steps.

NEXT STEPS

I am positive that you can create the "rest of your life" responsibly so that you die thoughtfully.

I'm not trying to guilt trip you; please believe me! There have been times in my life when I wanted to put down all my responsibilities, much less continue to ponder the mystery of being alive and, at some point, "crossing the veil."

What keeps me going when I experience setbacks? I return to that feeling I described after my father died, of knowing that we had done all we could for him. I want my loved ones to experience that, and the only way that will happen is if I do the work to prepare us all for that unavoidable and heart-breaking event: my death. That's why I am here to guide you now that you're ready for the next steps.

There are those who launch themselves onto this path because of a traumatic experience, but I don't want that to be what spurs you to action. Are you still feeling some reluctance? It's challenging to be at the forefront of cultural change, and being open to these conversations marks you as a trailblazer. You've got the basic steps in place by reading this book, so let's keep going.

It really makes no difference where you are in life right now as to whether this is the right time to move onto this path. Everyone over the age of 18 can benefit, but many wait too long until it's a crisis. They miss out on the opportunity to put plans in place when there's plenty of time to consider all the ins and outs.

What's in the way? Staying stuck in that mindset of:

- » I'm too young to think about the end of my life.

- » I'll do something about it someday, just not today.

- » I have plenty of time; after all, my parents lived well into their 80s!

- » There's no time in my life for this and I'll get to it when things calm down.

» I want to live for today, and thinking about the end is depressing.

» [Add your excuse here!]

You're not alone if you recognize yourself in one or more of these statements, trust me. But I don't want anyone to experience that extreme level of suffering my family went through because my mom didn't take her responsibility seriously.

Again, I'm not mad at her. I understand the circumstances of her life *and* her death.

If I didn't have the contrast between those two deaths, I wouldn't have created my *Experience Peace of Mind Now* program (more on that at the back of this book).

I also wouldn't have the sacred memories I carry that sustain me in those times when I miss my parents deeply. And I wouldn't have the serenity of knowing that my loved ones will have that peace of mind after I'm gone.

The blocks you think are in your way can be swept aside when you follow the steps laid out in this book. Now that you're aware that you've avoided the idea of death and you've subdued your resistance to the idea that it will certainly happen to you, you're ready to be accountable and take responsibility.

At this point, you have a few options.

Before going there, let's take a moment to get present. I invite you to close your eyes or just lower your gaze. Raise your shoulders as you breathe in deeply through your nose, then smile gently and blow your breath out, letting your shoulders drop. Make sure your feet are flat on the floor, and take another breath, feeling yourself grounded and connected to the planet. Blow it out again and invite in a sense of calm.

Picture yourself having created a roadmap for you and your loved ones to follow, and notice how you're deeply connected to yourself and those around you. You know what matters to you, and they can support you through to the end.

Ahhhh!

You may be intrigued but still not yet ready to venture out on this path. If that's you, check out my YouTube channel called the *End of Life Lounge*. You'll find engaging videos on a variety of topics that lead you gently into this amazing world of acceptance of your mortality.

(And keep reading, there's bonus content below.)

Okay, so now, what's next?

Path #1: Dead end here (pun intended!).

Doing nothing at this point is an option, and some may choose to go no further. You could close this book right now, decide that death is a problem for future you, and continue to live your life like it will never end. Unfortunately, this is how many people end up dying irresponsibly and leaving their families with additional burdens.

Because you've made it this far, however, I believe that you recognize a part of you that wants to get this behind you so you can focus on where you're going from here. Doing that without the baggage of avoidance is so much easier and more enjoyable!

Can you imagine how much lighter you'll feel when you know that you've defined your wishes, had conversations, organized your affairs, and done the work to lay out your roadmap? Getting the series of little tasks done opens you up to a whole new approach to life.

What happens if you do nothing? Not to be a downer, but if you're "lucky," you'll live for a long time, and in those years, you'll experience inevitable downturns that cause crises and up-end the lives of those around you as you all scramble to react. That creates stress and lasting trauma among those you love. Or, you might have a heart attack and die suddenly, leaving others to make decisions as they grieve their loss.

If that is the last thing you would want, then let's move on to your next option.

Path #2: Set out on the journey alone.

Your second option is to try and figure all of this out independently. If you've made it this far, then you know by now what the consequences of avoiding this work could look like. In this book, I've discussed many of the actions that you can take to not only die thoughtfully but live the rest of your life with intention.

I was a DIY person, too. I can say confidently that it can be done, but there are many things I didn't even know that I didn't know. I wasted time and money when I could have put those resources to much better use.

This is why I strongly encourage you to consider option 3.

Path #3: Consult your compass, and let's go!

On this path you choose to seek the guidance of someone who has not only been where you are but has also helped others to create peace of mind and a life of integrity.

Have you been unable to put this book down for the last hour, and you now realize that this is what you've been waiting for? I'm so excited to invite you to reach out and book a complimentary call with me. Let's explore what it would look like for me to be your guide on this path to living responsibly.

After all, it can be overwhelming to figure all this out on your own (that's basically what I had to do), so please take advantage of my experience (and mistakes). You don't have to wonder if you've covered all the bases, and it doesn't take years to put your roadmap in place. I can't wait for you to feel at peace!

Learn more and schedule your call with me at www. livingresponsiblyroadmap.com. That's where you'll also find my Living Responsibly Quiz, a quick, free, and illuminating self-assessment that I developed to help you determine if this path is right for you.

This is sacred work we are engaged in, and I would be honored to be your guide.

HOW I'M LIVING
RESPONSIBLY

It's now been 17 years since my mom died, and more than 5 years have passed since I lost my dad. The shock of being an "adult orphan" hit me hard at that point, but I still wasn't ready to make the choice to get my roadmap in place.

It took losing my job to light that fire under me.

There I was in late 2019, happily traversing Washington State, visiting different school districts to present de-escalation workshops to educators and administrators. Then came 2020 and the pandemic. When schools shut down, I was suddenly out of work. I couldn't believe the stories I read of so many people dying in hospitals, with loved ones unable to be with them. I had those treasured memories of supporting my dad through his end of life, and couldn't imagine the anguish those families were going through. That's really when I took Step 1: Conquering Avoidance.

With time on my hands, I began to dream about what to do next. I started the process by combining all my experience, talents, and passions and envisioning what legacy I could create. It was a real wake-up call for me to see all those lives cut short. What would I do with the time *I* had left?

That got me to Step 2: Overcoming Resistance to Our Mortality. With all the thousands of lives lost due to the pandemic, I had no choice but to look at my stubborn reluctance to engage with and accept the fact of mortality. The experiences I'd had with the deaths of my parents and others gave me confidence that I could work with others to get through these crucial first steps. With a background of over 30 years in education, plus my coaching and leadership experience, it made sense to find a way to help others see the reality for themselves.

Now the rubber hit the road: Was I actually going to make sure that my kids and sisters didn't have to go through what we experienced with my mom? I knew deep in my heart that I didn't want that to happen. I much preferred the outcome of feeling at peace after losing my dad, so I set to work to encapsulate the process into something that I could do and that would benefit others. I took it upon myself to get my affairs in place, and that's when I completed Step 3:

Being Accountable.

So what is there beyond getting your roadmap in place, with the checklist done and the conversations completed?

The rest of your life!

Yes, you have time ahead of you, no matter how short or long, and this is Step 4: Living Responsibly. I've shared some client outcomes with you, and you'll notice that living responsibly looks different in each case.

For me, it looks like bringing this vital work to as many people as possible. I do this by creating opportunities for people at all stages to step onto the path with me as they are ready; after all, each of us is one-of-a-kind.

You've heard about some of the ways I do this already. I also enjoy speaking to groups whether they be large gatherings of professionals, a book club with five members, or anywhere in between. I've worked with churches to offer group workshops and with senior centers to create ongoing community conversations.

It was a lovely surprise to find out that I have mediumship capabilities, and that would not have happened if I hadn't done this work. I've completed training with Suzanne Giessmann, who is an accomplished practitioner and an amazing teacher. The first spirit to come through was "Uncle Charlie," and I will forever be grateful to him and the client I was working with at the time. She was so surprised and delighted to hear from him, and it gave her closure to a challenging loss that had dogged her for years.

I've created a beautiful home for myself in a lovely community on an island in the Pacific Northwest where I can walk to pretty much anything I want. I have time and space for gardening, volunteering, and enjoying visits with my adult children and their partners. These are the values I discovered that matter most to me as I developed and applied my process.

I've been intentional about having conversations that will inform my kids and my siblings of what brings me comfort for minor as well as major incapacitations and, of course, for when the end of my life nears.

When I am gone from this body, I know that they have a guide for how to honor my life and will do their best. I like to think that they will continue to feel my presence in some form as I lift off into whatever is next.

Planning brings peace of mind, and my deepest wish is for you to have that experience.

Blessings!

ABOUT THE AUTHOR

"Life is just a chance to grow a soul." - A. Powell Davies.

Johanna Munson is a highly practical and deeply spiritual pathfinder whose soul-centered leadership brings you peace of mind through "Rest of Life" planning. As a Peace of Mind Guide and the CEO of End of Life Resources, LLC, she supports adults in facing inspiring and challenging decisions and conversations around who and what matters most. Struck by the contrast in how she felt about her parents' very different deaths, she put the lessons learned to good use and created her Experience Peace of Mind Now program.

Johanna is a lifelong educator and a licensed Willow End-of-Life Educator® and communications coach. She brings her deep appreciation for the human capacity for continued growth to her work with clients. Her path to the fulfilling life she now leads includes time as a stay-at-home mom, a Japanese language teacher, and an out-of-work trainer looking for what was next. The quote above reflects the approach she takes to all the ups and downs of life.

She enjoys gardening with her neighbors on a beautiful island in the Pacific Northwest, spending time with her two grown children and their partners, continuing to deepen her relationships with her sisters, and hopes to adopt a middle-aged dog soon.

ACKNOWLEDGMENTS

This book is the culmination of numerous interactions and experiences over the entire course of my life, and these are a few of the wonderful people I'd like to thank.

To my parents for always supporting my intellectual curiosity and for giving me the gift of awareness that death can be done differently.

To my sisters, for persisting in creating new and deeper ways of relating as the decades pass.

To my in-laws, for their deep and abiding love that taught me to live and forgive.

To my children, for bringing joy and fulfillment to my life.

To my wonderful clients, for continuing to inspire me in this work.

To my teachers, too many to name, but especially Lashanna Williams, Marie Manuchehri, and Suzanne Giessmann, for opening up new worlds to me.

I thank the wonderful team at AFGO Media & Publishing: Lin Eleoff, Dustin Dixon, and Rhianon Paige. It's been a delight to work with you all!

With gratitude,
Johanna

EXPERIENCE PEACE OF MIND NOW

Planning brings peace of mind. If you want to find someone who knows the ins and outs of "rest of life planning" based on personal experience and rigorous research and development, Johanna Munson has created a comprehensive program that addresses the Heart, Soul, and Mind of creating a personalized plan.

It's called *Experience Peace of Mind Now.* Here's what it looks like:

> » You'll identify who and what matters most to you (your values) as a foundation.

> » You'll determine your priorities and apply your values to action items so that you check off every box on the checklist we provide you.

> » You'll make decisions regarding health care wishes, current and future lifestyle, the actual end of life,

and more that reflect your values, and share them with those who need to know now so that there are fewer surprises.

Best of all, you'll rest easy knowing that you and those around you are ready for whatever may come, that you can now live the life you envision, and that you will leave good memories behind when you are gone.

Go to www.johannamunson.com to learn more.

LIVE RESPONSIBLY, DIE THOUGHTFULLY

How to Navigate the Rest of Your Life with Intention and Grace

Johanna Munson

---

www.livingresponsiblyroadmap.com

www.johannamunson.com

Visit Johanna's YouTube channel here:
www.youtube.com/@endoflifelounge

Join Johanna's Facebook group here:
www.facebook.com/groups/endoflifelounge

Contact Johanna at: hello@johannamunson.com

Published by AFGO Press

AFGO Press is a division of AFGO Media and Publishing, whose mission is to support women in building their own businesses.

For more information, go to AFGOmedia.com

Made in United States
Troutdale, OR
07/26/2024

21532518R00065